We need the sea.
We need a place to stand and watch
and listen—
to feel the pulse-beat of the world
as the surf rolls in.
—*David Brower*

Island in Time

The Point Reyes Peninsula

By Harold Gilliam
Photographs by Philip Hyde

Sierra Club/Charles Scribner's Sons • New York

Second revised edition.

Designed and produced in New York by
Charles Curtis, Inc. and Lori Joseph.

Printed and bound in Italy by Mondadori
Editore, Verona. Library of Congress
Catalogue Card. No. 73-6438. International
Standard Book No. ISBN 684-13439-X.

Preface

WHEN the first edition of *Island in Time* was published by the Sierra Club in 1962, one of its purposes was to call attention to the existence of this nearly pristine peninsula near San Francisco. Another was to demonstrate a need to preserve the peninsula. In that sense, it was a campaign book. A copy was placed on the desk of every member of Congress, and I would like to think that the book played a role in the passage of the legislation creating the Point Reyes National Seashore.

But there were other purposes. One was to sharpen the reader's visual perceptions of the woods and meadows, hills and dunes, cliffs and beaches, lakes and streams. This was the role assigned to photographer Philip Hyde, and the new pictures he has taken for this edition will further heighten the reader's sensitivity to the shapes and colors of the existing landscape.

The book was also intended to describe the extraordinary dimensions of time that may be perceived on the peninsula—geologic, biologic, and historic time. Unless the visitor gains some insights into these dimensions, he misses the greater part of the Point Reyes experience. However, in the years since the book first appeared, another dimension of time has been added. Even a superficial knowledge of it will contribute immeasurably to the depth of the experience there.

This new dimension of time is reckoned not in centuries or eons or epochs but in man-days of work; in toil, tears, and sweat; in the energy and devotion of Congressmen and their staffs, Interior Department officials, Sierra Club and conservation leaders, and above all thousands of volunteer workers who collected signatures, pushed doorbells, stuffed envelopes, answered phones and did the gruelling routine work that resulted in the birth of the National Seashore and its precarious post-natal survival. The visitor to any area of the National Park System—or to state and local parks—normally has no notion of this human dimension, but without it the parks would not be created and many simply would not continue to be.

Probably no park area anywhere has gone through more traumas or has depended more on the work of legions of volunteers than this one. Part of the turmoil stems from the fact that Point Reyes and its Atlantic coast counterpart, Cape Cod National Seashore, were the first units of the National Park System to be created by Government purchase of private property. Previous parks had been carved out of the public domain or, like nearby Muir Woods National Monument, had been received as gifts. Even after the Point Reyes legislation was enacted, private activities continued—many of them destructive to the purposes of the park.

Although the accompanying photograph of President Kennedy signing the authorizing legislation on September 13, 1962, to all appearances shows a victory celebration, there is a measure of irony in the image. Standing immediately to the President's left (holding a copy of *Island in Time*) is California Representative Clem Miller, chief author of the bill, who had a summer cottage at Inverness and, with his wife and five daughters, had explored the peninsula for years. Looking over Miller's right shoulder is Senator Clair Engle, who piloted the bill through the Senate.

A month after the picture was taken, Miller was killed in a private plane crash while visiting his district in Northern California. President Kennedy was assassinated in Dallas a little over a year later, and Senator Engle died of a brain tumor the following year. All three had believed that the Point Reyes Peninsula was secured for all future time. As events turned out, it was far from secure.

The signing of the bill did not mean the park automatically came into being. It had to wait for congressional appropriations and subsequent purchase of the land. Meantime loggers continued levelling the Douglas fir forest on Inverness Ridge. Speculators bought up land scheduled for Government purchase. Subdividers built roads and sold lots. For some months before the signing houses had continued to go up, built by people who were assured by realtors that if the Government ever got around to buying the property it would pay them handsome prices. And the prices soared, indeed.

As a result, the $14 million belatedly made available by Congress to buy the authorized 64,000 acres and some further small appropriations were used up before half of the land could be purchased. In park circles Point Reyes became a classic example of the devastating effect of rising land prices.

In 1969, faced with White House reluctance to spend more money for parks—and the unlikelihood of Congress voting more money over Administration objections—the National Park Service reverted to a strategy of desperation. It proposed to sell off for controlled private development, including subdivisions, some of the land it had already bought, in order to get cash to buy the remaining critical areas.

The proposal caused consternation in California and set off a Save-Our-Seashore campaign, supported by the Sierra Club and headed by energetic former Marin County Supervisor (later State Senator) Peter Behr. After a hardfought crusade, including a flood of letters to the President and Congress and half-a-million signatures on petitions, the Government found an extra $38 million to finish buying the entire 64,000 acres.

But even then Point Reyes as a natural island of serenity was still in danger. In 1965 the National Park Service had developed a master plan for Point Reyes that raised the hackles of conservationists. It proposed $35 million worth of construction, including a clifftop highway; conversion of the wildlife lagoons at Limantour Estero into a roaring motor-boat harbor, and the use of the magnificent dunes on Limantour Spit for shops, a pier, and huge parking lots—a kind of Jones-Beach-on-the-Pacific.

Fortunately the plan could not be carried out at the time because the property was not yet acquired. By the time the land had all been bought, the nation had discovered "ecology" and there was wide public support for the idea of maintaining the area's natural environment.

In 1971 the National Park Service proposed a second master plan more in accord with the spirit of the times. It recognized the value of preserving a maximum of the rare natural landscape and stated clearly the chief remaining threat to the park—the proliferation of automobiles carrying the anticipated 2,350,000 visitors a year. Acres of asphalt for roads and parking, car noise, and air pollution hardly seem compatible with the need for urban residents to experience nature directly.

But the Park Service's proposed new plan, labelled a "conceptual plan," was short on details and on commitment. It did not indicate, for example, how people were to be transported to and within the park without their deadly automobiles. Until there are provisions for a public transportation system to get visitors to the park from Bay Area population centers, the park will continue to be in danger of auto strangulation.

Another problem is the park's status as a National Seashore, which permits intensive recreational development along the lines of the abortive master plan of 1965. There is growing sentiment for the idea that Point Reyes should have the greater protection afforded by a change to the status of a national park.

There is increasing support also for protection of the peninsula's wilder reaches under the strongest shield available in law: the Wilderness Act. By 1973 the Park Service was supporting a wilderness area of 10,600 acres in the Mt. Wittenburg and Lake Ranch-Double Point areas. The Sierra Club and allies advocate Wilderness Act protection for some 34,000 acres including, in addition, the vulnerable esteros, the aquatic habitats of Tomales Point, Point Reyes Beach, Point Reyes Headland and the southern woodlands to Pablo Point overlooking Bolinas Lagoon. Congress will decide the issue.

Ultimately, however, no paper arrangements can provide adequate protection against inevitable pressures for intensive development. Lasting protection can come from only one source: continuous and energetic action by private citizens. Fortunately, late in 1972 there occurred a propitious event that provided a channel for citizen action.

As a result of a grass-roots campaign similar to that which created and protected Point Reyes National Seashore (a campaign headed this time by Dr. Edgar Wayburn and Amy Meyer), Congress and the Nixon Administration established the Golden Gate National Recreation Area adjoining Point Reyes on the south and east—34,000 acres of superlative shoreline on both sides of the Golden Gate. The bill authorized the appointment of a 15-member citizens commission to advise the National Park Service on four contiguous National Park units—the new recreation area, Point Reyes, Muir Woods National Monument, and Fort Point National Historic Site.

The mechanism is available; what is now required is the will, the energy, and the sensitivity to natural values displayed by those originally responsible for the park. Here is another reason for public understanding of the human dimensions of this peninsula. To name the people responsible and to narrate their struggles in detail would require another book as long as this one. Only a few can be mentioned here, but perhaps the list should be headed by Clem Miller, whose devotion to this peninsula and whose legislative skill were preeminent in the park's creation. Katharine Miller Johnson, his widow, and William Duddleson, his talented legislative assistant, have ably carried on his interest in the park. Sonya Thompson and Jim Eaton have designed the Sierra Club's wilderness proposal; Jerry Friedman perseveringly has defended the Seashore's natural places, and Anne West has set in motion the Seashore's first public transportation system—a modest van shuttle-service for hikers.

The list should also include Conrad L. Wirth, who had proposed a park here nearly 40 years earlier and who, as Director of the National Park Service, had helped bring the idea to fruition; George L. Collins, then of the National Park Service regional office in San Francisco, who suggested the idea to his friend Miller and guided the project to success locally; Stewart L. Udall, then Secretary of the Interior, and his Under Secretary James K. Carr; and David Brower, then Executive Director (now Honorary Vice President) of the Sierra Club, who was a leader in the Point Reyes campaign and who originally conceived and edited this book.

For invaluable help in preparing the book my thanks go to Geologist Alan Galloway and Botanist John Thomas Howell of the California Academy of Sciences; Robert H. Becker of the Bancroft Library; James Cole and Robert Lunty of the National Park Service; Joel Gustavson of the Point Reyes Foundation; the late Mr. and Mrs. B. K. Dunshee and their associates of the Marin Conservation League.

I owe particular thanks to Stewart Udall, who gave this book a high-level send-off and as a consequence of its original publication gave me the opportunity to spend a year with him in the office of the Secretary of the Interior. There I learned at first hand the complexities of conservation politics and acquired vast respect for the administrative and legislative leaders who are able to translate conservationists' good intentions into political reality.

As always, my ultimate gratitude goes to Ann Lawrence Gilliam, my co-explorer of the region, whose keen perceptions have immeasurably sharpened my own.

I would like to dedicate this new edition of *Island in Time* not only to Clem Miller and others responsible for this preserve but to the hope that their intentions will be carried out. To do so will require unending vigilance by men and women, living and not yet born, who are determined that this shoreline shall be eternally preserved from all encroachments.

HAROLD GILLIAM

San Francisco, April 1973

Photographer's Note

THE MOST visible and impressive change apparent at Point Reyes now, as compared with a decade ago, is the widespread enjoyment of the area by the public. One day last Spring, my family and I took a bicycle ride up the Bear Valley Trail. It was the day before Memorial Day, and as we wheeled back down toward Olema in the afternoon, the trickle of backpackers and bicyclists we had been with earlier swelled to a torrent. Whole families were taking off for a weekend in the country, carrying their life-support systems on their backs. The woods were filled with the happy cries of children—and grownups—enjoying their Seashore. As I watched them wending their way toward the beach through flower-filled meadows and woods whose tree-tops faded into fog, I was transported back to that road as I drove it in 1960, in my old pickup, through cow-filled meadows, over a private ranch road down to the brink of the ocean cliffs and along a dirt track north that ended near what is now Coast Camp. That was one of those rare days when all of that great white arc of cliffs that line Drake's Bay was visible. The cows were not only in the meadows, but scattered everywhere on the hills along the coast. The only biped around was me—with my tripod and camera.

In the Publisher's Foreword to the first edition of this book, David Brower asked the question: "Whose wild shore?" The answer came only after Point

Reyes became a National Seashore. Looking back thirteen years gives emphasis to that accomplishment.

To a misanthrope, perhaps, this shore was wilder in 1960 than in 1972, if you can overlook what cows can do to the land when there are too many of them there too long. But somehow, in 1960, I sensed the presence of the great metropolis that lies a scant forty miles away, and the land seemed too empty. I grew up in the heart of that metropolis, and my boyhood memories are still sharp of the sparseness of things green in city streets. I still recall my delight at finding a bit of moss or a blade of grass springing up in cracks in the sidewalk. And I remember long walks across a citywide expanse of hard pavement to reach the then unclaimed wildness of the Daly City Hills. Point Reyes was a distant and infrequent goal for family picnics then, and the Sunday drive ended with a long wait in the ferry lines at Sausalito.

Returning home after World War II, Point Reyes was one of the first places I revisited. I might not have been able to articulate the reason then, but I know now it was because it was still remote, wild-seeming and little changed. I remember passing through familiar Marin County made unfamiliar—metamorphosed in those war years by shipyards and extensive housing projects. But beyond the urban spread, Point Reyes was still much the same as it had always been: austere in fog, brilliant in occasional sun, remote, quiet though the metropolis next door had doubled in size. As I went back to school, then got absorbed in my life work and moved away from San Francisco, Point Reyes was all but forgotten until the day in 1960 when I joined a Sierra Club-Park Service tour of the Peninsula. That day we saw the results of logging just begun on the slopes of Inverness Ridge, and the start of subdivisions in several places on the shores. What had "always been there" suddenly seemed to be going fast, and it was clear that if nothing was done, the Peninsula would disappear under development, or behind private property signs. That day was the beginning of my participation with my camera in the drive to establish the Seashore. Since then I've been back a number of times, finding something old and new with each visit.

The waves beating on the Great Beach, or sliding up the long sand slopes under Drake's cliffs, always speak to me of the thread of change beneath the surface of all things. The "eternal" rocks wear down, or disappear. Walking along the edge of Drake's cliffs one day last Fall, I sensed something missing as I looked down on the beach. After some time I finally realized that a series of long, parallel rock outcrops that prominently thrust into the wave-line in my 1960 photographs were no longer visible, covered with sand brought up the beach by the restless waves. Awareness of such natural change heightens the fascination of this land-and-sea meeting place.

And in 1973, I'm grateful that this is one of the places on Planet Earth where the natural forces can go on in their own design, relatively unmolested by man's urge to make nature into something else. In that sense, our new edition of this book is a celebration of efforts, past and future, to keep the Point Reyes Peninsula unspoiled, an Island in Time, providing enjoyment and inspiration for generations to come.

PHILIP HYDE

Taylorsville, Calif., March 1973

Drake's Estero

Harbor Of The Golden Hind

FROM THE CLIFFS at the entrance to Drakes Estero on a clear day, you can look down the curving line of the white cliffs along Drakes Bay, where big green swells roar into breakers and charge toward the beach, their crests whipped into white banners of spindrift by the northwest wind. Beyond the estero entrance for three miles to the east, the waves break on the white sands of Limantour Spit, and occasionally in storms roll entirely across the long sand bar to the quiet waters of the estero inside.

Directly below you, on the near side of the channel, another, shorter sand-spit extends from the foot of the cliff, partly enclosing a cove a couple of hundred yards in diameter. In all the miles of cliffs, dunes, ridges, lagoons and white beaches visible from here, little has changed as yet since the days of the sixteenth-century explorers. A sense of history lingers about this place, for here in the cove at your feet is a focal point for one of the most intriguing mysteries ever to surround a historic event.

Is this cove below you the lost harbor of Francis Drake? Can this be the spot historians have sought for generations—the place where the great explorer landed in California on his historic voyage around the globe—forty-one years before the landing of the *Mayflower* at Plymouth Rock? Did he careen the *Golden Hind* on these sands, erect his stone fortification near the foot of this cliff, and leave here his plate of brass claiming this land in the name of Queen Elizabeth? Are these the white cliffs that reminded Drake of the English channel and caused him to name this land New Albion?

In June of 1579 Drake was sailing south down the California coastline carefully looking for a special kind of harbor. Having plundered the Spanish settlements in the New World on his voyage up from Cape Horn, he was anxious to avoid running the gauntlet of the Spanish galleons, by now looking for him in force. He would take care of the Spanish at a later date and in another ocean in one of the greatest naval engagements in history. Now it was time to return home to England with his treasure.

Having sailed north along the coast and failed to find the fabled Northwest Passage around the top of the continent, he concluded with characteristic daring that the best way home was across the uncharted Pacific. His tiny *Golden Hind*—less than 100 feet long—was not in condition for such a voyage. It would have to be careened, refitted and repaired, a very delicate operation involving completely unloading the vessel and hauling her up on some protected beach in a position invulnerable to storms. Such sheltered harbors are rare on the rugged Northern California coast and Drake doubtless considered and rejected several harbors en route before making his selection.

The accounts of the voyage compiled some years later from notes taken by Francis Fletcher, Drake's chaplain, indicate that on June 17 the *Golden Hind* sailed into "A faire and good Baye, with a good wind to enter same." After probing the bay's shores with a small boat for three days, Drake found a good site for the careenage, not far from a creek with an ample supply of fresh water. Uncertain as to the kind of reception he would get from the Indians, who were watching from the cliffs, Drake ordered his men to erect a stone fort on the beach. The fort proved unnecessary, however, as the Indians were highly hospitable. The crew of the *Golden Hind* went to work on the vessel, hauled her into shallow water and over a six-week period made the necessary repairs. Drake and some of his men made a short hike into the interior, took possession of the land in the name of Queen Elizabeth and sailed away.

Until late in the last century, it was generally assumed by both British and American historians that Drake had sailed through the Golden Gate and careened the *Golden Hind* in San Francisco Bay. Then local research by historian Hubert Howe Bancroft and scientist George Davidson threw considerable doubt on the assumption and led to the theory that the historic landing had taken place in what is now known as Drakes Bay. Other historians lined up behind such California harbors as Bodega, Tomales, and Half Moon bays. And innumerable Californians, fascinated by the Drake mystery, lined up behind the historians or developed their own favorite theories, which they defended with a passionate zeal. As a Piedmont matron has remarked: "You'd better know how people feel about Drake when you're making out your guest list for a dinner."

The most controversial piece of evidence is an inset map of the "lost harbor" of New Albion drawn by the Dutch cartographer Jodocus Hondius a dozen years or more after the voyage. Part of a global map of the Drake voyage, the inset is designated "Portus Nova Albionis," Drake's landing place in California. It pictures a horseshoe-shaped bay bounded on the left by a peninsula, with an island beyond.

Both amateur and professional historians have tried to fit the Hondius map like a piece of a jigsaw puzzle to various places on the California coastline. George Davidson believed that the map was a portrayal of Drakes Bay and the peninsula was Point Reyes. He was unable to explain the island, however, except as one of the offshore rocks of Point Reyes which the map maker had enlarged and misplaced. Historians who have identified the "portus" as Bodega Bay, north of Point Reyes, have also been unable to explain the island satisfactorily. Skeptics claim the map does not represent any real location but is probably a fanciful drawing by Hondius—his own idea of the way the port might have appeared. Historian Robert Becker even finds a new location to which the map could apply—Tom's Point on the east side of Tomales Bay. "The drawing," he concludes, "can be applied to a number of different locations, even to one heretofore overlooked, and . . . the sketch itself is at best only corroborative evidence."

Nevertheless the search for the Hondius harbor goes on. Amateur historian Robert Powers, owner of the Nut Tree restaurant near Sacramento, is certain that the peninsula depicted on the Hondius map is the Tiburon Peninsula, inside

Drake's Bay

San Francisco Bay, and the island alongside it is Belvedere. The map's bay he identifies as the northern part of San Francisco Bay, under the assumption that San Pablo Strait, not shown on the Hondius map, would not have been visible to the map maker.

The Hondius map must be considered in conjunction with various other clues to the landing place. One is the latitude of the harbor, not mentioned on the map. The accounts differ slightly in this respect, one account giving it as 38 degrees and the other as 38 degrees 30 minutes. Conceding possible error in ascertaining latitude, the harbor could be expected to be within a degree of the 38th parallel, which passes through both Drakes Bay and northern San Francisco Bay. Bodega, Tomales, and Bolinas bays would also qualify.

Another clue is the climate, described in Fletcher's account as exceedingly frigid for summer. The accounts mention "nipping cold" and ". . . thicke mists and most stynkinge fogges. Neither could we at any time, in whole fourteene dayes together, find the aire so cleare as to be able to take the height of sunne or starre." Such weather conditions might be found at any of the coastal bays but are far less likely inside San Francisco Bay.

Fletcher was evidently unhappy with the terrain as well as with the climate: ". . . How unhandsome and deformed appeared the face of the earth it selfe, shewing trees without leaves, and the ground without greenes in those moneths of June and July."

Yet on a brief exploration inland from the harbor, the Englishman found that the scenery changed rapidly: "The inland we found to be farre different from the shoare, a goodly country, and fruitful soyle, stored with many blessings for the use of man."

The immediate area of Point Reyes and Drakes Bay is certainly devoid of lush vegetation, and the "goodly country" inland could well be a description of the Olema Valley region just over Inverness Ridge. Yet the Olema Valley would have also been accessible from Bodega or Tomales bays.

Probably the strongest evidence favoring Drakes Bay are the white cliffs, which bear a striking resemblance to those of the English Channel. "Our Generall called this Countrey, Nova Albion, and that for two causes; the one in respect of the white bankes and cliffes, which lie toward the sea: and the other, because it might have some affinitie with our Countrey in name which sometime was so called."

It is argued by partisans of San Francisco Bay as the landing place that this statement did not necessarily mean that the white cliffs were at the harbor itself but since they "lie toward the sea" might have been seen as the *Golden Hind* passed them en route to a harbor inside the Golden Gate.

A further clue to the location can be found in the encounter between the Englishmen and the Indians. There were Indian villages near the harbor and dozens of curious natives came to see the bearded white men. As soon as the *Golden Hind* entered the bay a single Indian paddled out to the vessel in a canoe and delivered a long unintelligible oration to the Englishmen. Later he returned twice, bringing gifts of feathers. The crew of the *Golden Hind* offered him trinkets in return, but he refused to accept anything but a British hat, which he donned with great pleasure and paddled away.

Later on the shore the Indians presented more gifts of feathers, quivers,

Bishop Pine, Inverness Ridge

and "the very skins of beasts that the women wore on their bodies." Simultaneously they showed great excitement and agitation. The women, virtually hysterical, deliberately lacerated and bruised themselves severely.

Evidently news of the arrival spread rapidly. During the six-week stay of the *Golden Hind*, Indians arrived from miles around. At one point a tall Indian, obviously a chieftain, clad in an elaborate coat of hides, appeared with a procession including women with baskets of food. Drake invited the chief, who was called Hioh, into his stone fortification with the members of his retinue, who performed songs and dances. One of the Indians, evidently the chief orator, "wearied both us his hearers and himself, too, with a long tedious oration, delivered with strange and violent gestures, his voice being extended to the uttermost strength of nature, and his words falling so thicke . . . that he could hardly fetch his breath again."

As the climax of the ceremony the chief placed a crown of feathers and bone on the head of Drake, an act interpreted by the English as yielding up the right and title to this land to Queen Elizabeth.

From Fletcher's description of the ceremonies, houses, and adornments, as well as Indian words that he reported hearing, anthropologists have concluded that the tribe was the Coast Miwok, who inhabited Marin county and part of Sonoma County south of the Russian River. This narrows the search somewhat but still includes Bodega, Tomales, Drakes, Bolinas, and San Francisco bays.

One piece of evidence, however, seems to point to Drakes Bay in particular. The odd behavior of the Indians indicated that they considered the Englishmen to be the dead returned to life. And among the Miwoks, Point Reyes was considered the abode of the dead.

The most renowned piece of evidence regarding Drake's landing is the famous plate of brass, which was unearthed by a picknicker in 1936 on the shore of San Francisco Bay near San Quentin. The plate, appropriately inscribed, was believed to be the one that Drake's men had nailed to a "greate and firme post" at the harbor of the *Golden Hind*. Although there are still skeptics who consider the plate an expert forgery, chemical tests seemed to indicate that it was genuine. Its discovery near San Quentin focused the search for Drake's landing place once more on San Francisco Bay. Then the chauffeur of a San Francisco banker declared that he had found the same plate three years earlier on the shore of Drakes Bay about four miles east of the estero entrance, had carried it around in his car unaware of its value and had finally thrown it out near the spot at San Quentin where it was subsequently picked up. Although some authorities were skeptical of the chauffeur's story, it was cited by partisans of Drakes Bay as confirming evidence for their theories of Drake's landing place.

Another clue to the location of the lost harbor is a reference in the accounts to offshore islands, which could only be the Farallones. The *Golden Hind*, repaired and fit for the Pacific voyage, sailed out of its snug harbor on the 23d of July, to the weeping and wailing of the Indians, who ran to the hilltops and lighted fires, watching the vessel disappear on the horizon. "Not far without this harborough did lye certaine ilands (we called them the ilands of Saint James) . . . having on them plentiful and great store of Seales and birds, with one of which wee fell July 24, whereon we found such provision as might completely serve our turne for a while."

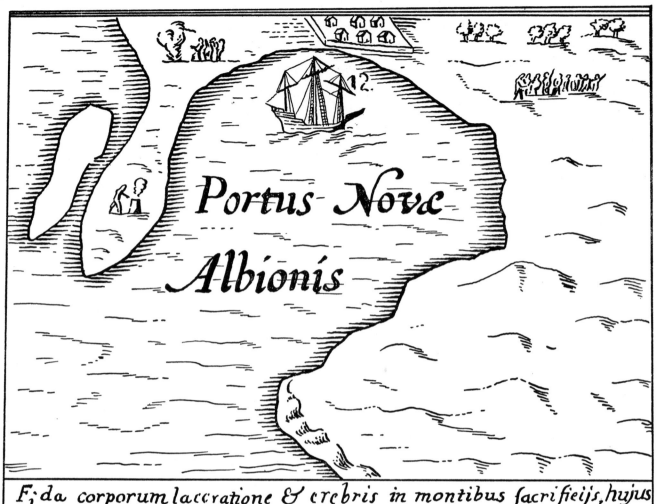

Fida corporum laceratione & crebris in montibus sacrifieijs, hujus Novi Albionis portus .incol . Draci. jam bis coronati . deceßum deflent.

GMC

Above is the Hondius map of the California harbor where Drake careened the Golden Hind. Conceivably this is a map of the cove just inside the entrance to Drakes Estero, as indicated on the opposite page, although the Hondius map must be almost inverted if it is to match. Other differences may be explained by the recent silting up of part of the cove and the frequent changes in the positions of the sand bars at the entrance, which at certain times have resembled Hondius' peninsula and the adjacent island. A comparison of the map on the opposite page with the end-paper map in the front of the book illustrates the continual changes that take place in the shape of the estero entrance.

The phrase "not far without this harborough" might be taken to narrow the alternatives down to Drakes Bay and San Francisco Bay. The Farallones are a group of rocks and islands about 30 miles west of the Golden Gate Bridge. The nearest of them is some 20 miles south of Drakes Bay. Much is made by partisans of both bays of the point that the *Golden Hind* set sail on one day, July 23, and arrived at the islands the next day. The islands would hardly seem a day's sail from Drakes Bay but might well be a day's sail from some harbor inside the Golden Gate.

Those who favor Drakes Bay point out, however, that it was customary navigation practice at the time to measure a day from noon to noon; the ship could have sailed from Drakes Bay in the morning and arrived after noon, which would technically be the next day. But San Francisco Bay partisans retort that while a ship's log might have used the noon-to-noon basis for computing days, a journal such as Fletcher's would have held to the more common practice of measuring the day from midnight to midnight.

Thus do the contenders spin out their theories in minute detail, piling elaboration on elaboration in confusing array. One further point should be noted regarding the islands. Because of the Farallones' rugged cliffs, the only one of the islands on which Drake's men would probably have been able to land was the Southeast Farallon, the largest of the group, which is equidistant from Point Reyes and the Golden Gate.

Even among those who consider Drakes Bay as the most likely landing place, there have been differences of opinion as to the precise spot on the shore where Drake may have careened the *Golden Hind*. Many historians tended to follow scientist George Davidson, who believed that the careenage had taken place just inside the inner tip of Point Reyes on the site of the present Coast Guard docks. But no thorough investigation of possible alternate sites was made until 1949.

In that year a group of Bay Area boating enthusiasts organized the Drake Cruise, an annual yacht excursion from San Francisco Bay to Tomales Bay. Curious as to the details of the Drake landing, they began to dig into the records, organizing themselves into the Drake Navigators Guild to pursue the study. Among them were M. P. Dillingham, a sales engineer; Adolph Oko, a former sea captain; F. R. Brace, an electrical engineer; and Robert Marshall, a Drake's Bay rancher. Fleet Admiral Chester W. Nimitz later became intrigued with the problem and joined the search, contributing valuable navigational information. Much of the research centered around the map that had puzzled scholars for generations, Hondius' "Portus Nova Albionis."

After years of effort, the research began to pay off. Pieces of evidence turned up in odd places. In a bookshop at the top of the Spanish Steps in Rome, Oko turned up a document published in 1638 confirming the account of a Portuguese pilot who had been with Drake. In the Science Museum in London he found valuable data on 16th century ships and navigation. Dillingham was thumbing through an old issue of the *National Geographic* when he came across a picture of a traditional careenage port in the West Indies which led him to investigate the whole subject of careening ships. He learned that the harbors used for that purpose were invariably small, protected areas. And he learned that the word "portus" was commonly used to designate a protected inner harbor near the mouth of a river or estuary.

Cobweb thistle

Thus the search was narrowed. Most of Drakes Bay, including Davidson's favored location, did not seem to match conditions required for the delicate work of careening the ship. But there did seem to be one location that fit the requirements—Drakes Estero, the inner lagoon or drowned valley, protected by the sand bars from the direct impact of the surf.

The Drake Navigators combed the many miles of shoreline. Guild member Raymond Aker, a maritime expert, noticed that the configuration of the sand bars around the mouth of the estero changed at various times. He began to delve into the principles of sand bar formation and noted with increasing excitement that from time to time, alongside the spit immediately west of the entrance, the changing currents created sand islands. At times their shape approximated that of the island on the Hondius map.

With this discovery the parts of the puzzle seemed to fall into place. Drake's men had built a stone wall "at the foot of a high hill"—evidently the steep hill just above the sand bar. Although the hill was just off the map, Hondius did portray Drake's tents enclosed by the wall. There is ample loose rock in and around the cove to have supplied material for the fortification. It is even conceivable that some of these rocks are the scattered remains of the wall. Or perhaps the wall still exists, buried beneath the shifting sands.

The members of the Drake Navigators Guild are convinced that the Hondius map corroborates their study of Drake, of Elizabethan navigation practices, and of all the other evidence relating to the voyage. For them there is only one possible conclusion: The filled-in cove just inside the entrance to Drakes Estero is the lost harbor of the *Golden Hind,* Portus Nova Albionis, New Albion, the original New England, site of the first English landing in this country, the Plymouth Rock of the Pacific Coast.

Partisans of San Francisco Bay as Drake's landing place, however, maintain that the evidence compiled by the Navigators Guild is inconclusive and fails to explain, among other things, how the plate of brass happened to turn up on the hillside by San Francisco Bay underneath an apparently ancient pile of rocks—which may be the very pile that originally supported the "greate and firme post" to which the plate was nailed by Drake.

Doubtless the controversy will continue to vex historians, both amateur and professional, and complicate the plans of dinner hostesses for generations to come.

Unless, perhaps, someone strolling along a lonely beach should stumble across the ruins of an Elizabethan rock fort, exposed by shifting sands . . .

Headlands

Stacks

AS YOU WALK up over a slight rise near the seaward mouth of Bear Valley there is a sudden rush of wings directly ahead, and you are startled by the shrill scream of a red-tailed hawk. The big bird rises over the chaparral of the ridge, circles slowly, dipping to reveal his rufous-red tail feathers, screams again, and sails out of sight over a ridge.

You walk across the old wave terrace carved by some ancient surf but now 30 or 40 feet above the ocean. The broad shelf of land extends along the coast above the cliffs as far to the north as you can see. To your left is a narrow gorge, carved deep into the terrace by the creek flowing down from Bear Valley.

As you reach a point of land bound on two sides by cliffs, you can see the sand beaches below and several large sea stacks just offshore, relics of the former coastline. The coastal hills, their crests shrouded now in fog, seem to be rising through the mists of time as they once rose to new heights above the sea, rolling back the ocean, lifting this wave terrace far above the level of the waves that created it. Now the surf is carving out another terrace below, cutting back the cliffs, leaving offshore these sea stacks, obdurate masses of rock that the waves have not yet been able to consume.

On the largest of the stacks is a scene that seems to belong to the primeval mists that roll over these hills. Around the lower part of the rock are perched dozens of black, long-necked cormorants, primitive birds that seem to have risen from the water like the first flying reptiles of evolution. Frequently they return to their natural element, diving below the surface for minutes at a time, emerging with a furious beat of wings, tails trailing in the water, before rising into the air.

On top of the big rock stand several birds not far from the cormorant in the scale of evolution—huge brown pelicans that are graceful in the air but absurdly ungainly on land. As you watch, one of them lifts its long bill into the air and stretches its wings like some Jurassic pterodactyl, half bird, half reptile.

Down in the gorge to your left, where the stream has sliced its way through the old terrace formation, you can see along the walls the edges of inch-thick strata once laid down on the sea bottom, dozens of layers warped and curved by pressure and stacked one on top of another like bent plates. Where some of them have been broken away, there are natural rock gardens planted with portulaca and lupine.

Surprisingly, you notice that the bottom of the gorge, which contains a considerable flow of water upstream, is dry at the point where it opens on the beach. Curious as to how the entire stream can disappear in so short a space, you clamber from the point down the steep rock wall to the bottom and follow the water as it flows around a bend.

There the mystery is heightened. The creek suddenly abandons its course and pours into a natural tunnel in the rock beneath the point on which you had just been standing. Stooping and peering into the tunnel, you can see what has happened. At the far end of the tunnel, the stream meets the incoming waves from the other side of the point. The tunnel was evidently hewn out by the waves attacking the far side of the point and eroding their way through the rock wall to the stream-cut gorge.

Doubtless the tunnel is continually being enlarged and in time will become an arch between the point and the mainland. Then, over the millenniums, as the rock is eroded away, the arch will collapse and the tides will flow entirely around the point, turning it into a sea stack like those offshore.

And so in the perennial war between the sea and the land, the sea will continue to wear away this edge of the continent until such time as the crust buckles again, the land rises or sinks or the sea level changes, creating a new shoreline, beginning again the ancient rhythmic cycle.

Wreck Of The San Agustin

JUTTING SHARPLY INTO THE OCEAN far beyond the general line of the coast, this peninsula is a natural hazard for ships. In three and a half centuries some 50 vessels have piled up on the rocks and beaches of this wild shore. Of all the shipwrecks that have taken place on this rugged coastline, none was more dramatic than the first.

In 1595, sixteen years after the *Golden Hind* sailed away across the Pacific, the Spanish galleon, *San Agustín,* loaded with treasure from the Orient, stood down this coastline. Her master, Sebastian Cermeño, a Portuguese, was grimly dedicated to a special mission. Spanish authorities in Mexico had commissioned him to find good harbors along this coast as ports of refuge for the Manila galleons, the vessels that sailed annually from Acapulco to the Philippines in the Orient trade, returning with favoring winds across the North Pacific and down the California coast.

The *San Agustín,* herself one of the Manila galleons, arrived on this coast battered and leaky after a long, stormy voyage across the Pacific, low in the water with 150 tons of oriental cargoes. The crew, forced to devote two out of three watches to manning the pump, was nervous about the condition of the vessel. The officers, fearing for the safety of the galleon, tried unsuccessfully to persuade Cermeño to skip coastal explorations and proceed as quickly as possible to Acapulco. They took every measure short of mutiny, serving on Cermeño a written demand that he sail straight home.

But the hard-bitten Portuguese commander had no intention of abandoning his mission. Risking mutiny, he insisted on proceeding with the exploration. Following the coastline southward, he sighted a high ridge extending into the ocean and swung his *San Agustín* around it into a protected bay. From Cermeño's exact description, it is evident that the ridge was today's Point Reyes and the harbor was Drakes Bay. His account mentioned a river flowing into the bay—doubtless Drakes Estero, which resembles a river estuary. He found a good supply of fresh water flowing into the estuary at the head of Home Bay.

For three weeks Cermeño camped at Drakes Bay. He named the coastal indentation between Point Reyes and Point San Pedro, south of the Golden Gate, "La Baya de San Francisco."

Although accounts of Cermeño's encounter with the Indians indicate that they behaved similarly to those encountered by Drake and were doubtless Coast Miwok, the natives gave no indication that they had ever seen white men before.

Drake's Beach

Spiderweb

On the beach at the estero entrance—possibly the same place Drake had careened the *Golden Hind*—Cermeño's men assembled a launch, the parts of which had been brought from Manila, for the purpose of exploring the shoreline more closely than would be safe with the bulky galleon. The launch was simply a large dugout log with planks along the sides.

Unlike Drake, Cermeño was in this vicinity at the stormy season of the year. His galleon was not taken into the protected estero—possibly because of the difficulty of navigating the shallow entrance. It was anchored off the entrance to the estero, completely unsheltered from southerly winds. A November gale came up suddenly from the southeast at a time when most of the crew was ashore. The *San Agustín* was ripped from her moorings. Despite the desperate efforts of the few men aboard, the galleon was driven toward the beach. Her hull hit bottom in shallow water and she wallowed helplessly, pounded by giant breakers. Each comber acted as a battering ram and within a few hours the *San Agustín* was pounded to pieces. Several crewmen and a priest were drowned.

It is not difficult to imagine the state of mind of the crew as they stood on that lonely foreign shore, their vessel destroyed, several comrades dead, with only the clothes on their backs and the launch on the beach. There is no record of what mutinous thoughts may have entered their minds, what eloquent Spanish oaths they may have directed at their captain, whose stubbornness they held responsible for their plight. Evidently they decided to suppress their fury under the assumption that their chances of survival with their tough commander would be better than without him.

Even so, Cermeño had a hard decision to make. There were three possible choices: He and his men could remain here and take up life with the Indians; they could try to walk down this unknown coast 1500 miles or more to the Spanish outposts in Mexico; or they could all crowd into the launch and take their chances of getting back to Mexico through stormy winter seas. Perhaps because he felt more at home on the sea—even in an overcrowded open boat— than in the wilderness of this unknown land, Cermeño elected the latter course. He set his men to work collecting food from the unappetizing stores of the Indians—acorns, wizened fruit and seeds. When they discovered some Indians taking planks from the wreck, a fight ensued. But they might as well have let the Indians have the remains, for there would obviously be no room in the launch for the scattered treasure of *San Agustín*.

When the surf was sufficiently calm, the launch was shoved from the beach into shallow water and 70 men and a dog jammed into the open vessel, which rode dangerously low in the water. Doubtless crowds of incredulous Indians watched from the beaches and cliffs of Drakes Bay as the unwieldy little vessel set out on its forlorn and almost hopeless journey. Doubtless, too, there were few of the 70 men aboard the strange craft who expected to see home again. The only good omen was the name of the launch—the *San Buenaventura*. The saint was a medieval philosopher, but the literal meaning of "buenaventura" is "good luck."

The dugout sailed south from Drakes Bay, passing inside the Farallones but keeping a safe distance from the rocky shoreline. The crew members were so busy navigating and checking the seaworthiness of their vessel that they failed to see the break in the coastal hills that opened into the greatest natural

Driftwood, The Great Beach

harbor in the New World. For another 170 years the Golden Gate and the great bay remained hidden.

Cermeño's southward journey was one of the most harrowing sea voyages in history. The starved crewmen were driven to eat the dog and might have started on each other had they not found the carcass of a large fish that had washed ashore on an island. The doughty *San Buenaventura* lived up to her name. The tattered, gaunt men of Cermeño arrived in Mexico in January of 1596. Doubtless they were grateful to have arrived home, but held Cermeño responsible for their ordeal. Years later the pilot, Francisco Bolaños, bitterly wrote that "The loss (of the *San Agustín*) was caused more by the man commanding her than by the force of the wind."

The Indians at Drakes Bay were delighted to claim the wrecked cargo of the *San Agustín*. Probably they pulled planks from the wreck to use in their own houses, and for years afterward slept on the silk that had been destined for European royalty and ate their acorn meal from Ming porcelain that was worth more than gold.

Three and a half centuries after Cermeño's disgruntled and fearful men launched their little craft in the surf off the estero, archeologists headed by Dr. Robert Heizer probed the sites of Indian villages at Drakes Bay and found more than 100 fragments of Chinese porcelain plates and bowls identified as pieces from the Wan Li period of the late Ming dynasty (1573–1619). Along with the porcelain they unearthed 65 iron spikes of the kind used in construction of the wooden ships of the time.

Theoretically, both the porcelain and the spikes could have been left by either Cermeño or Drake. Yet Drake would hardly have given the extremely valuable porcelain to the Indians. And Fletcher's account indicated that the Indians scrupulously returned the gifts that were presented to them by the Englishmen. Cermeño, on the other hand, was forced to leave everything behind. It seemed to the archeologists more likely that the unearthed material was part of the wreckage of the *San Agustín*.

The members of the Drake Navigators Guild dispute this conclusion. They point out that the spikes could have come from either the *Golden Hind*, as a result of the repairs that were made, or from a captured Spanish bark Drake left behind at the Nova Albion anchorage.

As for the porcelain, the Guildsmen speculate, it might have been left behind by Drake, despite its value, to lighten the *Golden Hind* for the dangerous Pacific Crossing. Or it might have been spilled from a small boat unloading the *Golden Hind* for the careenage operation. Furthermore, it is a matter of record that the *Golden Hind* carried porcelain, whereas there is no record of such a cargo aboard the *San Agustín*.

The arguments either way are far from conclusive. Perhaps the decisive evidence—some identifiable fragment of treasure—still remains hidden somewhere in a drift of sand along Drakes Bay.

Birds

DRIVING ALONG Sir Francis Drake Highway near the upper end of Tomales Bay, you catch a glimpse of something white at a distance out in the marsh. You stop the car just in time to see one of the most rewarding sights in the world of wildlife.

A hundred yards away a big white American egret, standing close to four feet in height, slowly spreads its wings, circles briefly over the marsh and alights a short distance away. In that quick flight of a few seconds you behold a spectacle of unmatched grace and rhythm, a combination of planes and curves of wings, arched neck and tail feathers that would delight Euclid—or Degas. No ballerina, bound by the force of gravity, could approach the egret's superb, soaring grace, the symmetry and poetry of its motion.

You notice now that there are several of the big birds scattered across the marsh, their white feathers glinting in the sun against the rich ochre-brown of the grasses and the turquoise of the water in the channels, which flows swiftly inward with the tide, reflecting the morning sunlight.

There are other birds, as well: two smaller snowy egrets with crested plumes, and a single great blue heron, a huge crane-like, blue-gray bird even larger than the American egrets. All of them stand nearly immobile in the marsh with curved necks arched, facing in the same direction—into the breeze, bills slightly lifted as if in anticipation of something momentous about to arrive on the wind and the flood tide.

Near the other side of the marsh there is a sudden flash of spangled light in the air, just as suddenly vanishing and reappearing in a few seconds. It is a flock of small sanderlings darting above the marsh, visible when the white undersides of their wings reflect the sun, invisible a few seconds later when their dun-gray backs are toward you.

As you get back in the car, the quick scintillation is still before your eyes. Driving toward Inverness, you wonder how soon this scene will be destroyed by people who believe that a marsh has no value other than to be "reclaimed" —filled for long rows of the same kind of houses that spread for mile after mile along the shores of San Francisco Bay.

In our rush to develop more living space, will we leave any breathing space, any room for relief from dull suburban monotony? Will there be any place in the future for a sudden glimpse of marshland beauty, for the quick flash of the darting sanderlings, for the great blue herons and the breath-taking flight of the soaring white egrets?

Gulls, Lower Lake, Lake Ranch

Drake's Beach

Peninsular Eden

THIS "ISLAND IN TIME" offers perspectives into the geologic past and into the remote human past as well. Here on this peninsula are the remains not only of an ancient land mass but also of an ancient civilization. Along deserted beaches or the rolling uplands above Drakes Bay or down the piny draws of Tomales Bay you can see the remains—only mounds now—of a race of people who made their homes here for thousands of years.

At the time of the landings of Drake and Cermeño, there were probably more permanent residents on the peninsula than live there at the present time. Anthropologists have discovered the sites of 113 aboriginal villages. They have unearthed broken shells, left-overs from many an Indian meal, arrowheads that once brought down some of the peninsula's abundant deer, pieces of mortars and pestles used for grinding grain, clam disk beads, stone jewelry, tubular pipes, whale-bone wedges—all indicating that the Indians had developed a well-organized culture.

Although technologically they might be regarded as primitive, in at least one respect their civilization surpassed our own: there was no pattern of organized warfare. Unlike most of mankind, including Indians of other parts of the country, the Coast Miwok lived in harmony among themselves and with other tribes. Their friendliness and hospitality surprised the Englishmen of Drake and the Spaniards of Cermeño. Their ceremonies on meeting the Europeans indicated a well-developed pattern of ritual.

The peaceful pattern of Indian culture no doubt reflected their environment—a land of abundance. Food was no problem. The waters were full of fish and the sands were thick with clams to be dug at low tide. Great flocks of birds came down to the water, and deer and small game were plentiful in the hills.

The Miwoks had developed techniques of removing tannic acid from acorns and had dry granaries for storing them. They fashioned tule canoes to paddle in the lagoons; Drake and Cermeño were both greeted on arrival by a welcoming committee consisting of a single man in a canoe.

Across the uplands and along shores where the soil is not too sandy, there are still visible occasional shallow saucer-shaped pits in the ground—the site of an ancient village. The houses were dug several feet into the ground and the walls above ground were built of driftwood, piled together in tepee shape. The fogs and winds were kept out by clay packed on the walls.

The Miwok—like other California tribes—were also far ahead of their time in another sense: they initiated the California custom of indoor-outdoor living.

Although they had nothing that could precisely be called a patio, they pioneered in the use of a kind of outdoor barbecue, preparing most of their meals just beyond the front door using elaborately woven watertight baskets.

Physically they were very powerful. Drake's men were awed with their ability to run long distances at great speed and to spear fish with deadly accuracy. Their robust health enabled them to face the cool winds of the peninsula with a minimum of protection. The usual costume of the men consisted of exactly nothing, except on ceremonial occasions when they were decked out with coats of hides. The women, wrote Drake's chaplain, Francis Fletcher, wore a skirt of bulrushes, "which being knitte about their middles, hanges downe around their hippes, and so affords to them a covering of that, which nature teaches should be hidden: about their shoulders they weare also the skin of a deere . . ."

In another respect the Miwok housewife was quite modern: she took great pains with her hairdo and head ornaments, using shells, bones and feathers in ingenious coiffure designs.

With the arrival of the colonizing Spaniards, the ancient culture of the Miwok came to a sudden end. In 1817 Mission San Rafael was established and the Franciscan fathers proceeded to proselytize Indians all over southern Marin county. The recruitment was extraordinarily successful. The villages were abandoned, the entire peninsula was left uninhabited, and the culture was gradually forgotten as the Indians took up agricultural life under the padres at the mission.

Mission San Rafael lost its power by 1834 when all the missions were "secularized" by the Mexican government. Without the guidance of the padres, the Indians were helpless to organize their own communities, and even in a scant 17 years had evidently been away from their native environment too long to return successfully. A few of the Indians did drift back to their original homes, but many more were rounded up by ranchers for use as virtual slave labor. Rapidly they died of disease and starvation and within a short time only a few miserable survivors were left.

Of the culture of the peace-loving, energetic people who welcomed Drake and Cermeño, the only remains are the desolate mounds where once their villages stood on shores and rolling downs of this time-haunted peninsula.

Pond, Lake Ranch

Limantour Spit

Colonizers

FOR MORE THAN A CENTURY after the coming of the Americans, this peninsula, which was once the site of a flourishing Indian culture and which figured prominently in the earliest explorations, was largely bypassed by the tides of progress. Although close to the booming center of population and commerce around San Francisco Bay, the peninsula has remained very sparsely inhabited, situated as it is over mountain roads winding away from the main north-south arteries of travel.

Less than a decade after the discovery of gold the entire 100-square mile peninsula, with the exception of the northern and southern extremities, was purchased from the few settlers by Oscar and James Shafter, San Francisco attorneys. For more than 60 years the Shafter family operated dairy ranches on most of their land and leased out the rest for the same purpose. And for nearly three-quarters of a century the peninsula's dairy products were hauled by schooners from wharves in Tomales Bay and Drakes Estero to San Francisco. In the 1920s the transport job was taken over by trucks and the schooners sailed into limbo, although some of the wharves remain.

The oldest settlement on the peninsula is Bolinas, which in Spanish times was a harbor for American, British, and Russian ships engaged in the sea-otter trade. During the Gold Rush it became a center for timber logged in the hills behind it and shipped to San Francisco from Bolinas Lagoon. When the town declined as a lumber and shipping center, it became a week-end retreat and vacation refuge, consisting mainly of summer homes.

Shortly after the beginning of the timber operations above Bolinas, some enterprising businessmen discovered outcrops of limestone on the west side of Olema Valley about five miles north of the head of the lagoon. They dug a quarry and built several lime kilns, but the venture was unsuccessful. The kilns remain, however. Because of the fact that some large Douglas firs are growing almost on top of the ovens, a legend developed that the kilns had been operated by the Russians who had a colony at Fort Ross, 50 miles north, from 1812 to 1841. Recent borings in the trees, however, indicate that the largest—about three and a half feet in diameter—dates from the 1870s.

The village of Olema began in 1857 as the Olema House, a combination store, saloon, and hotel. The present Olema House, still standing at the northeast corner of the crossroads, was built in 1877.

Although the members of the Shafter family were interested primarily in ranching, they did not completely overlook the peninsula's scenic attractions. In 1889 James Shafter set aside 640 pine-covered acres on the west side of

Tomales Bay for the resort village of Inverness, which was developed for campers, fishermen, and vacationers. The scenic qualities of the peninsula were also noted by some members of San Francisco's exclusive Pacific Union Club, who leased land in Bear Valley, constructed a country club there in 1892 and secured hunting and fishing privileges on adjacent ranches. The club became a renowned social resort for a time but was disbanded in the 1930s and the buildings were subsequently destroyed. In the 1920s and '30s the Shafter lands were gradually sold off; many of the ranches went to tenants who had been leasing them.

For more than a century the waters around this peninsula have been important to fishermen. Since the 1890s Drakes Bay has been used by fishermen bringing in salmon and other catches to unload there rather than make the long trip into San Francisco Bay. Wholesalers took the fish from there to the city first by boat then by truck. Crab boats haul in large quantities of the crustaceans from the shallow waters of Drakes Bay and nearby offshore areas. There are oyster beds both in Tomales Bay and Drakes Estero, identifiable by the long fences protecting the beds from predatory fish; here Japanese oysters are seeded and grown. Minus tides find amateur clamdiggers on the sands at Duxbury Reef and Drakes Estero. Waders and skin divers pry red abalone from the rocks around Tomales Point. Quantities of rockfish, ling cod, sea trout, and other fish are hauled in by sport fishermen operating from skiffs in Tomales Bay.

Because of its isolation the peninsula has been found ideal for overseas radio transmitting and receiving facilities. The maze of poles and wires eight miles north of the point itself is the RCA and AT&T combination of "receivers" for voices coming over radio telephone from the Orient and Australia. Just north of Bolinas is an RCA transmitting station.

Since the wreck of Cermeño's *San Agustín,* half a hundred ships have come to grief on the rocks and beaches of this peninsula. In 1870 Point Reyes lighthouse was built on the tip of the promontory 300 feet above the surf, one of the most spectacular lighthouse locations on the Pacific. The three-ton lens, consisting of more than 1,000 pieces of glass, was made in Paris, brought around the Horn in a sailing ship, and carried to the point by oxcart. Until 1939 the intricate lens, combined with a small gas flame, emitted a 120,000 candlepower light. The coming of electricity in that year stepped up the beam to half a million candlepower and made the light visible 24 miles at sea. The light is maintained by the Coast Guard, which also has a rescue station just inside the inner tip of the point.

Drake's Beach

Wind, Fog, And Sun

THE VARIOUS KINDS OF TERRAIN on this peninsula—the beaches and cliffs, the rolling downs and salt water marshes, the lakes and streams and deep forests and wooded coves—are matched by the variety of its weather. On many days it is possible to go from the windy fogbound seacoast to pleasantly sunny valleys, woods, and beaches only a few minutes' drive away—and to experience the entire range of weather between the two extremes. During the summer, sunbaked residents of the Sacramento and San Joaquin valleys find relief in the cool seaside climate while visitors from foggy San Francisco can relax on warmer inland beaches and in wooded dells.

The promontory of Point Reyes itself, thrusting boldly into the ocean beyond the general shoreline, is the scene of some of the most spectacular weather in the nation. It bears the full brunt of winds and storms that sweep across the wide spaces of the Pacific and strike the continent with a mighty impact. In winter storms the roaring surf around the outer point batters the rocks with a force that seems to shake the windows in the old lighthouse. Giant combers explode into sheets of spray and geysers that sometimes rise 100 feet into the air.

There are few more impressive beaches on the continent than the unobstructed eleven miles of strand north of the point—particularly when mammoth breakers from Pacific storms thunder ashore with a sound like an artillery barrage.

In the summer the promontory is a focal point for another distinctive phenomenon that affects the entire coastline. The prevailing winds, blowing from the cool Pacific toward the warm inner valleys of the continent, are deflected rightward by the rotation of the earth and strike the slanting California coast from the northwest. The winds moving on the face of the water create strong ocean currents. Pushed by the wind, the surface of the offshore waters flows massively south in a broad current like a river down the coast.

But this ocean river, too, is deflected to the right by the rotation of the earth and the surface waters tend to move away from the shoreline. As they do so, cold waters from the sunless depths rise to the surface to replace the waters that have drifted offshore. As a result of this upwelling, the waters along the coast of northern and central California are colder than the waters along any coast of the United States outside Alaska.

When the onshore winds blow across this cold streak and are themselves cooled, the moisture they have collected in their long sweep across the Pacific often condenses, forming a fog bank many miles wide which blankets the coast

McClure's Beach

south to Point Conception. Usually the cycles of fog alternate with cycles of sunshine throughout the summer.

Jutting out into this coastal fog bank, Point Reyes is often enshrouded in rolling white mists, and the reasonant bass roar of the foghorn sends a warning out to passing ships miles at sea. The foghorn is operated on the average of 1493 hours per year—the equivalent of 62 days. Sometimes only the tip of the point itself is enshrouded. At other times, particularly in late afternoon, the fogs drift inland over the rolling dunes and across the marshes, flowing up the seaward canyons in long sinuous fingers or in masses and wraiths of mist that envelop the upland pines and firs, tree by tree and grove by grove.

Often the fog is confined to the ocean side of the peninsula, but sometimes advance salients rise high enough to overtop Inverness Ridge and move down into Olema Valley in rolling cascades. Another tongue of fog may enter the mouth of Tomales Bay and penetrate southward. Oddly, although the point itself is one of the coolest places in the U.S. (outside Alaska) in summer, it is unusually warm in the winter. The temperature of the point is moderated by the ocean around it, which changes very little in temperature during the year. There is less than a four-degree difference in average winter and summer temperatures. On the average there are only three days a year at the point cold enough for frost to form.

On occasion, winter storms with winds exceeding 100 miles per hour have assaulted the point. The average year-round wind velocity at the lighthouse, however, is 11.5 miles per hour, rated on the Beaufort Scale as a "gentle breeze."

Inland from the point the wind diminishes sharply. One evidence of variety of weather conditions to be found on the peninsula is the shapes of trees. On the slopes near the ocean the pines and cypresses are often bent into permanently contorted shapes by the wind. Inland, away from the ocean winds, the bishop pines on the shores of Tomales Bay and the Douglas firs on the uplands of Inverness Ridge grow to magnificent proportions.

Living Relics

POINT REYES PENINSULA is an "island in time" botanically as well as geologically. Wander among the groves of dome-topped bishop pines that grow along the slopes above Tomales Bay; watch the ghostly wraiths of summer fog drifting through the foliage where the sea wind has fashioned it into weird primeval shapes, and you may be convinced that you have stepped several million years back into time.

The impression is well founded. This forest is a relic of that part of Tertiary time when most of California was sea bottom and this peninsula was an island—part of a great archipelago that stretched southward for hundreds of miles. Wherever these rare relic pines—or their cousins the Monterey pines—are seen along the coastline in scattered groves, there was one of the islands of this ancient chain, now part of the mainland.

East of the San Andreas Fault in this area, the dominant tree is the redwood, and here the fault is the boundary between redwood country and bishop pine country. Occasionally seeds of one or the other tree drift across the fault and attempt to gain a foothold in alien territory but neither tree will thrive in foreign soil. There are a few such expatriate bishop pines on the mainland near Lagunitas Creek and a single small redwood grove on the Point Reyes Peninsula in the Olema Valley a few miles north of the head of Bolinas Lagoon. Normally, however, the fault boundary is well observed. The bishop pine thrives in the granite and there the redwood cannot successfully compete with it.

Although high on Inverness Ridge and for a short distance down the windward slope the two-leafed bishop pines are hewn into fantastic shapes by the prevailing breeze, along the protected shores of Tomales Bay they grow to impressive size and sometimes their dome-shaped tops interlock to form a continuous roof. Strangely, the trees in any particular grove often seem to be all about the same size and age. The explanation lies in a curious characteristic of the tree. The cones, which grow, oddly enough, not on the ends of the limbs but encircle the trunk and branches at intervals, do not open annually to spread the seed but remain closed for many years, usually until they are opened by heat. Thus a forest fire will cause millions of long-hoarded seeds to be scattered, reforesting the ashy slopes with a crop of trees all the same age. Very hot weather may have a similar effect. Sometimes in the spring and fall when the hot dry winds blow from the northeast, you can hear the crackle of the opening cones all day, even into the night.

To the south along Inverness Ridge the granite does not lie on the surface as it does above Tomales Bay, and there the pines give way to the tall Douglas

Bishop Pines near Inverness Ridge

fir—the Black Forest. Except where some areas have been logged over in recent years, this is a virgin stand, in truth the forest primeval. Beneath the towering Douglas fir are the broadleaf trees—live oak, laurel, and tanbark oak, and in some spots where rainfall is particularly plentiful, ranging up to 55 inches (compared with 18 along the coast) the ferny undergrowth reaches jungle-like density.

Among the rare plant life of the peninsula are six specialized varieties that grow nowhere else in the world. Particularly notable is the Point Reyes ceanothus—a wild lilac that grows to tree-sized proportions at such favorable locations as Mud Lake, where it reaches 25 feet in height. Other common trees are the madrone, with rich red bark and edible berries, the buckeye, with torch-like blossoms in the spring, and the red alder, which grows abundantly along streams.

The brushy areas of the peninsula support such shrubs as toyon or California holly, wild roses, willow, purple nightshade, sage, and blackberry. And the grasslands in spring and early summer are streaked with wildflower displays that are among the finest of their kind in the United States. Particularly spectacular on the rolling grasslands in years of proper rainfall are many varieties of lupine, including *Lupinus arboreus*, a long-stalked plant with blue or yellow flowers, often tinged with lavender and purple. There are few more dazzling sights on the coast than the springtime fields of lupine and yellow-gold California poppies.

Obviously the abundance and variety of plant life on the peninsula makes the area highly hospitable to animal life, including great numbers of black-tailed deer, raccoons, foxes, bobcats, coyotes, and an occasional mountain lion. In a national bird count by the Audubon Society in December of 1960, 164 species were found on this peninsula and a section of the adjacent mainland—the second highest count of any equal-sized area in the United States.

In animal life as well as plant life, the peninsula harbors rare species. It is the southernmost habitat of the mountain beaver; the only place where that odd seabird, the California murre, breeds on the mainland; and the wintering ground for one of the largest concentrations of black brant geese on the Pacific Coast. It is one of the few areas where sea lions and harbor seals can both be seen, and there have been reports of an occasional elephant seal, a rare mammal weighing more than two tons.

This peninsula is a living museum not only of the processes that have shaped the crust of the earth but the wildlife that has evolved upon it—of plants and animals that elsewhere in this part of California have long since been displaced by the inexorable advance of pavement and tract houses.

Woods

FROM THE BIG rolling meadow at the high point of Bear Valley you stroll up a trail leading into the forest. A little more than an hour earlier you were in the city and the morning headlines were large and black with thermonuclear crisis, but here you are in another world. The sunlight sifts through the branches of the tall Douglas firs, falling through the lower oaks and laurels, making patterns of light and shade on the rich brown compost underfoot. You inhale the heady fragrance of the woods, dominated by the pungent aroma of the laurels, and experience a sense of exhilaration that contrasts sharply with the nervous, claustrophobic atmosphere of the world below.

At every bend of the trail is evidence of the life force in action. Just to the left of the path you come across a huge laurel with two trunks; one, five feet in diameter, stands erect; the other extends out almost horizontally in a long flat arch. From the horizontal trunk a dozen branches shoot straight toward the sky, each one large enough to be a fair-sized tree in itself.

Curious as to what produced this odd effect, you step closer, and the story becomes plain. The two trunks evidently were once twins with a common bole, perhaps having sprouted from the stump of an older tree. Many decades ago a gale ripped one of the twin trunks from its roots and sent it crashing to the forest floor. It was severed at ground level except for a few slim tentacles of root that still clutched the soil. Evidently this slim margin of life was enough. The root expanded and supplied nourishment to the fallen trunk. From its upper side new shoots sprouted, reaching up for the light. Now they are almost large and numerous enough to constitute a grove in themselves.

Life persists, although it does not inevitably triumph. Walking around to the other side of the tree you see an epilogue to the story. There on the ground is a fallen log that appears to have been a third trunk of the same tree— possibly felled by the same wind—long since dead and disintegrating.

You wander on up the trail, through the Douglas fir forest and the understory growth of shiny-leafed huckleberry, wild lilac, coffeeberry, monkey flower, and sword fern. Off to the left is a sudden blaze of bright orange-red where some kind of brilliant vine climbs the trunk of a tall Douglas fir. Looking more closely, you note that its shiny leaves grow in groups of threes. It is unmistakably poison oak, one of the most strikingly beautiful plants in the forest—when viewed with caution.

Inverness Ridge

Suddenly, far off through the woods, there seems to be the sound of a bird call, so faint that you cannot be entirely sure you heard it, so melodious that it stirs ancient memories. You stop and listen again, hearing this time only the twitter of some nearby sparrows.

Down the slope twenty yards away you encounter another odd-shaped tree— this time a Douglas fir. At ground level the trunk is six feet thick; then it spreads out and just above your head its diameter is close to 12 feet. From that point there rise four or five parallel trunks. Evidently the original leader was nipped by wind or fire—possibly about the time the *Golden Hind* was careened in some nearby bay—and from the wound grew half a dozen leaders, each of which became full-sized trunks in its own turn. The result is what appears to be several trees growing from a single trunk.

Ultimately, as you stroll down the forest aisles, your thoughts turn again to the tense atmosphere in the city below—to the grim headlines and the solemn voices. But somehow the dire prophecies do not seem as doleful as they did earlier. Something about the day—the sunlight filtering to the forest floor, the unending variety of vegetation, the innumerable forms of life in every square yard of these woods—gives you a sense of immense potential.

It occurs to you that what you have been seeing here in these woods is the continual fulfillment of possibilities, the manifestation of life's perennial ability to cope with adversity by means of ingenious innovations which themselves become the basis for new creative impulses, new advances in the scale of evolution. Perhaps here is the ultimate value of wilderness— of open space, of natural parkland; it enables us consciously or subconsciously to renew contact with life's incessant aspiration. And you wish fervently that all the statesmen in every country—and all those who make public decisions and judgments on the issues of our time—could wander frequently through such woods and hills as these, exposing themselves to the endless ingenuity and diversity of nature and to its infinite range of possibilities. Yet opportunities for such exposure are rapidly disappearing. A few miles from where you are walking, for example, acres of this forest have been leveled by lumbermen. And farther north along this same ridge, bulldozers are cutting a network of roads through the woods for a subdivision.

Rounding a bend in the trail, you startle several big black-tailed deer, who go bounding away in long leaps with a great crackling of the underbrush. The forest is quiet again for a moment. Then you hear once more the same far-off bird call. This time there is no doubt: It is the incomparable song of the hermit thrush, pure, clear and flutelike.

Forest, Inverness Ridge

Willet on Drake's Beach

Mounds

ON THE BEACH of a cove between the granite cliffs of Tomales Bay, where the bishop pines and the live oaks come down to the water, you can readily spot the dark mound where an Indian village once stood. The black earth is full of thousands of white shells thrown here by the villagers after dining on the clams, oysters and other shellfish that were abundant in the calm waters of this bay.

The beach is deserted now. As you sift the shell fragments through your fingers, you can almost hear the yells of the vanished aborigines as a flight of sea-birds alights on the water or as someone digging in the wet sand finds a particularly large bed of succulent clams.

The scene is easy to reconstruct: The huts of the village stand behind you on the beach above the high-tide level—conical dwellings dug several feet into the ground, walled and roofed by cone-shaped stacks of bark, saplings, and logs, plastered over with clay. Naked youngsters splash at the water's edge, shrieking with delight. Women chatter and sing as they work with woven baskets or prepare outdoor fireplaces for cooking. Some drink or scoop water for cooking from the creek that flows down this cove into the bay. A few men, unclothed and muscular, stand quietly on the rocks at the edge of the cove below the cliffs, watching the bay surface closely, occasionally darting a spear into the water to bring up an impaled fish. Others return from hunting expeditions in the pine forests, carrying game.

You can't avoid wondering, as you stroll around this ancient village site, what happened to the people who dwelt here in the sun by the placid bay. For hundreds or thousands of years their villages stood in these quiet coves. Hundreds of generations wove baskets, dug clams, speared fish, throwing the remains in such mounds as the one on which you stand. Then within a single generation they disappeared, their culture with them.

Evidently, like the individuals that compose them, cultures are mortal and succumb to similar causes—disease and age and violent death or slow attrition. Yet surely each individual who lived in this village in this cove between the pine groves and the flowing waters assumed that this culture would go on forever, that his children and his children's children would always weave baskets and fashion stone implements and spear fish and make bows and arrows to hunt along this shore.

You dust off your hands, leave the mound, walk slowly along the shoreline, wondering if some stroller on this beach centuries from now will pick up a broken beer bottle and in his mind picture the people who left it.

Pt. Reyes and The Great Beach from North Pt.

The Ephemeral Granite

LIKE THE LEGENDARY FLATLANDERS who live on a plane surface and have no conception of height or depth, most humans are oblivious to a dimension that exists outside their own experience: the vast reach of cosmic time in which all of human history represents but a fraction of a second.

Even the spans of time involved in the development of the solar system or the evolution of our own planet seem beyond conception. The imagination quails when we are told, for example, that the enduring mountains, symbols of permanence, are actually transitory features of a mobile surface, that parts of the crust of the earth rise and fall and move sideways like waves on the surface of the ocean.

Yet it is sometimes possible to transcend the boundaries of our own particular Flatland and achieve the beginning of a conception of that vast dimension of time. If we cannot actually enter that dimension, we can at least stand on the threshold and peer in.

There are certain locations on the surface of the earth that may be called threshold regions—places where the results of changes in the earth's mobile crust are dramatically visible.

Among the most notable threshold regions in North America are the Grand Canyon, Yosemite Valley, Yellowstone, the gorges of the Columbia. Of all such regions on this continent, there is probably none closer to a large center of population than the Point Reyes Peninsula. Here is a 100-square-mile living museum of the processes that are shaping the face of the planet.

THE SAN ANDREAS

The Point Reyes Peninsula is separated from the mainland by one of the most remarkable features on the earth's visible surface—the San Andreas Fault. The San Andreas, which caused the great San Francisco earthquake and fire, is one of the greatest continental faults on the crust of the planet. The largest movement along the fault on that fateful morning of April 18, 1906, took place not in San Francisco, where the fault runs offshore, but 40 miles north of the city, where the entire Point Reyes Peninsula was suddenly thrust northwestward in an immense grinding fracture. Near the village of Bolinas the thrust was about 13 feet. Farther north at the Bear Valley Ranch, it was 16 feet. And the greatest measured displacement along the entire fault was at the head of Tomales Bay, where the area west of the rift was instantaneously jolted 20 feet out of line. Roads, paths, fences, rows of trees were crazily pulled asunder.

From Point Reyes the fault extends northward along the edge of the continent some 160 miles before apparently veering out to sea near Cape Mendocino. It can be traced south of San Francisco, where it cuts inland then extends on southward along the Coast Range into the southern end of the state and disappears into the Gulf of California—a distance of some 700 miles.

This may be far more than the earth's greatest continental fault, however. Recent geologic discoveries indicate that the San Andreas may be a visible portion of one of the three primary features of the earth's crust. The first two are the oceans and the continents. Scientists probing the ocean floor in the past few years have discovered a third, a rift which extends downward entirely through the crust and runs one and a half times around the globe—a distance of 40,000 miles. Although most of this great rift is beneath the surface of the oceans, it slices along the western coast of North America as the San Andreas Fault.

The significance of this globe-girdling crack is only beginning to be understood, but some geologists believe that it may be primarily responsible for a hitherto unexplainable phenomenon of incredible magnitude—the apparent migration of the continents. It is this continental motion that has resulted in the drastic climatic changes that have taken place in geologic time. California—and particularly the Point Reyes Peninsula—is one of the few places on earth where the Great Rift leaves the ocean floor and becomes visible on land.

Here the motion along the Great Rift is lateral; adjacent portions of the crust slide alongside one another. One of the largest examples of lateral motion in historic times is on the Point Reyes Peninsula. The entire peninsula is moving northwestward—relative to the mainland—at a rate of about two inches a year.

This of course is an average rate. The surface motion is not steady but spasmodic. Deep in the earth, titanic blocks of the crust may be steadily shifting their position and placing strains and pressures on the surface blocks—pressures which build up until the rocks break with a shudder in an earthquake.

If this motion, at the average rate of two inches a year, has taken place continuously over the centuries, the peninsula has migrated about 65 feet since Francis Drake made the first European landing on this coast nearly four centuries ago. Since the first human habitation in this region a few thousand years ago, it has moved possibly ten times that distance.

No one knows how long this motion has been going on, but it is evident that the 1906 earthquake—which caused the maximum displacement of 20 feet—was only the most recent major movement in the history of the San Andreas.

THE SWALLOWED COW

In the weeks after that earthquake, the eminent American geologist Grove Karl Gilbert made an intensive study of the action of the fault along this peninsula. He found that along the fault zone from the head of Tomales Bay to the head of Bolinas Lagoon the earth had been broken into giant blocks or splinters. Everywhere in steep areas were landslides. Trees were uprooted or broken off. The earth was humped into ridges or broken in big cracks.

The greatest measured movement along the fault was at the head of Tomales Bay. The road crossing the fault there was depressed three and a half feet where it traversed the 60-foot-wide fault zone. The two ends of the road were left hanging; the west end was 20 feet farther north than the east end.

Drake's Beach

Dairy herd, Drake's Estero

Not far away at the Bear Valley Ranch, astride the fault, Gilbert found a row of raspberry bushes offset fourteen and a half feet. The path leading to the front door of the ranch house was fifteen feet out of line, as was a nearby fence. The milking had been going on just prior to the quake, and the cows and men had been thrown to the ground.

At the Shafter ranch near Olema one of the most curious events of the entire earthquake took place. "During the earthquake," Gilbert reported, "a cow fell into the fault crack and the earth closed in on her so that only the tail remained visible. At the time of my visit the tail had disappeared, having been eaten by dogs, but there was abundant testimony to substantiate the statement." Shafter's cow was the peninsula's only fatality.

Another freak result of the big shake took place near the top of Inverness Ridge. Mud Lake, a secluded tarn in the Douglas fir forest immediately west of the ridge line, was drained of most of its water. The only clue as to what happened was that a spring on the east side of the ridge three-quarters of a mile away suddenly increased greatly in volume. Since the quake, the lake has been restored by natural processes.

Many of the results of the quake spotted by Gilbert are no longer visible. The roads and paths have been straightened and the damage to the trees long since has ceased to be evident. But other evidence remains and is being unearthed by geologist Alan J. Galloway of the California Academy of Sciences, who has tramped over the entire area as part of a projected 20-year study of the geology of the peninsula.

Galloway has found that just as the 1906 quake was but a single episode in the long history of the San Andreas, so the crack in the surface created at that time is but one of a large complex of cracks and rifts, many of them centuries old, stretching along a belt half a mile wide. Along the entire zone are humped-up ridges, ponds with no outlets, odd escarpments, streams running in illogical directions, and a general jumble of earth features of many different ages where the surface has been fractured and crumpled over periods of hundreds and perhaps thousands of years. Although the age of the fault is reckoned in millions of years, all but the evidence of the past dozen or so centuries has been destroyed by erosion.

FAULT VALLEY

The most visible evidence of the San Andreas is the fault valley itself. The repeated shattering of the rock along the entire zone has left it highly vulnerable to erosion. Millennial rains have poured down on the fragmented material, washing it away and creating the long straight depression followed by Highway 1. At either end the fault valley has been so eroded away that it has been filled by the waters of the ocean, creating Bolinas Lagoon and the long narrow finger of Tomales Bay.

Driving along the fault valley from Bolinas north, you can see on every hand the evidence of this gigantic disruption of the surface. A half mile south of the road intersection at the head of Bolinas Lagoon, for example, a pre-earthquake house sits in a gully created by the fault. The 1906 quake knocked the house off its foundations but the sturdy frame structure was simply set back on concrete blocks and is still in use.

A half mile north of the same intersection a side road comes into Highway 1 from the west; 100 yards along this road you can look back to the northeast and see a section of the fault that looks like a road cut.

Six miles farther north on the right side of the road is a depressed area that in winter and spring is filled with rain water. This is a sag pond, created along an old portion of the fault where the land was depressed.

FREAK CREEK

At Olema a side road branches off to the west and leads to the Bear Valley Ranch, where Gilbert observed the damage in 1906. Here the 1906 fault gully runs along the right-hand side of the road, and just beyond the ranch gate in the chaparral to the right are the concrete markers erected in 1906 to gauge future movement along the fault. Another mile beyond the ranch buildings, at a point just before the road curves to the left, there is a fault scarp and gully about 20 feet up the hillside to the right.

Among the most curious evidences of faulting in Olema Valley is the strange pattern of stream drainage. For a considerable distance the valley is drained by two parallel streams flowing close together in opposite directions. Olema Creek drains the valley northward into Tomales Bay, and Pine Gulch Creek drains it southward into Bolinas Lagoon. For several miles they parallel each other a quarter of a mile apart.

The explanation for this freak condition is that each stream follows one of the valley's numerous cracks caused by earthquakes. Olema Creek, nearer the highway, follows the easternmost of the two fault traces. Pine Gulch Creek follows another rift to the west. The 1906 crack in this area was between the two, somewhat nearer Pine Gulch Creek.

The erosion of the long fault valley has created a series of short tributary streams flowing eastward down Inverness Ridge into the valley itself. As the valley has deepened along the fault, the streams flowing down Inverness Ridge into the valley have become steeper, flowed faster, and more rapidly carved canyons in the ridge. Some of them have cut their way upward into the headwaters of the older streams flowing down the opposite side of the ridge into the ocean.

This process has taken place most notably in Bear Valley. For about two miles up the narrow valley above the ranch buildings, the road follows a rapidly cutting creek, which flows back down the valley into the fault zone. Just beyond the headwaters of this stream, the road enters a rolling meadow-like clearing.

This surprisingly open area in the midst of a steeply contoured region is the remains of an old valley that once extended considerably farther north. Its northern portion has been cut into and eroded away by the creek which drains northward into the fault zone. The remaining part of the valley, however, is still drained by a stream running southward to the ocean. This latter stream once drained the entire valley in the days when the meadow was much larger—before the upper part of its drainage was "captured" by the more rapidly cutting stream to the north. In the same way all the creeks flowing down into the fault zone are fast cutting their way back into Inverness Ridge.

Another unmistakable feature of a fault zone can be noted in the fact that streams flowing into it from both sides make sudden right-angle turns as they intersect the fault cracks and proceed to flow along them.

Drake's Beach from Inverness Ridge

LANDSLIDES

The heavings of the earth's crust along the fault over the millenniums have created innumerable landslides. The largest of these is a monumental slippage on the west side of the peninsula that covers an area of several square miles. The ocean, cutting away at the foot of Inverness Ridge, undermined a large hillside region where the beds of sedimentary rock slope seaward. Earthquakes triggered the sliding of vast masses of rock and soil downward along the slope of the beds. Such slides have an odd quality of seeming to defy the force of gravity and at certain points rise upward into the air. What has happened here is that the front end of the slide struck an unyielding object in its downward path, possibly an unmoving mass of rock. Pressured by the sliding rock behind it, the front end rose upward above the obstruction. When the slide came to rest, the odd upward thrusts remained. Behind them were depressions that were gradually filled with water from the natural drainage and became the five gem-like lakes and numerous ponds of today's Lake Ranch.

All these upheavals and geologic oddities have been caused by the slow ponderous spasmodic drifting of the entire peninsula northwestward throughout the eons. Since the extent of the fault first became evident in 1906, geologists have searched diligently for an answer to the fascinating questions: How far has the peninsula moved? Where did it originate? Until recently many geologists have assumed that the total horizontal movement along the fault must have been not more than a few miles. Under this theory the peninsula would have "originated" someplace near the present site of the Golden Gate.

This is a piece of evidence that might have come in handy for the amateur theorists who believed that the reason early explorers missed the Golden Gate was that it was somehow hidden from their view. If the Gate was hidden, however, it was more likely to have been obscured by fog than by Point Reyes. If the peninsula ever did occupy that area, it did so at least some millions of years ago, long before the Gate itself was carved through the rising Coast Range by the Sacramento River.

More recently geologists have speculated that the movement along the fault may have been over a much greater distance. This speculation has grown out of efforts to match the peninsula like the missing piece of a jigsaw puzzle to the place on the mainland where it may have originated. Oddly the peninsula's bedrock granite did not match any similar rock east of the fault in central California.

The only matching granite along the San Andreas Fault was an incredible distance south in the Tehachapi Mountains. By radioactive measurements, however, geologists have learned that the Point Reyes granite measures out at the same age as the Tehachapi granite—about 80 million years. The conclusion is tentative, but considerable evidence seems to indicate that Point Reyes has been migrating for all of these 80 million years and has traveled some 300 miles.

VERTICAL MOVEMENTS

It would be wrong, of course to conclude that the peninsula as it exists today has made that long journey unchanged in size or shape. The forms of the land have gone through many metamorphoses over those eons, a fact attributable not only to erosion during the long horizontal journey from the south but to considerable vertical movement as well.

Beach near Lifeboat Station

72

This land has risen and fallen many times during its horizontal travels, sometimes totally submerging, sometimes consistently rising. The results of the more recent up-and-down movements are still visible in the form of ancient beaches high on hilltops, old wave marks on ridges, stream-carved canyons and valleys now submerged by the sea, and the appearance on ridge tops of rocks that were once laid down on the bottom of the ocean.

Geologist Galloway has drawn a set of diagrams to illustrate the dramatic rising and falling of the entire region as the crust continued to heave in response to pressures deep in the planet. The oldest rocks on the peninsula, now found in scattered locations along the top of Inverness Ridge, were originally laid down as layers of sand, clay and lime on the floor of a shallow sea some undetermined time in the geologic past (diagram A).

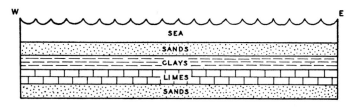

A. Layers of sand, clay, and lime were deposited in a shallow sea.

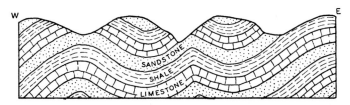

B. Sedimentary layers were compacted into soft rocks, then folded, and eroded when land mass was elevated above the sea.

C. Pressure and heat of molten granite which intruded the soft rocks changed them into hard metamorphic rock.

Over millions of years, the sediments were compacted into rocks—sandstone, shale, and limestone—and buckled by upheavals of the crust (diagram B). Then from deep in the earth came molten material that intruded the beds and solidified into granite some 80 million years ago. The heat and pressure of the granite metamorphosed the old sedimentary rocks into hard quartzites, schist, and crystalline limestone, which formed the "roof" over the granite, as shown in diagram C.

Then for more millions of years the land was slowly lifted until it rose above the sea. The roof beds were exposed to waves, wind and rain and in time most of them were eroded away, leaving the granite exposed. Some old roof rock remained as "pendants" in the granite (diagram D). Beginning about 60 million years ago, in the long rhythms of crustal movement, the land again subsided and was covered for some 50 million years by the ocean. Sea bottom sediments of sand and clay accumulated on top of the old formations (diagram E).

At the end of this period another elevation took place, and for the past 10 million years most of the area has been above sea level (diagram F). Once more the elements have eroded away most of the overlying beds, exposing the hard gray granite which is visible at Point Reyes, along Inverness Ridge (from Mount Wittenberg northward to Tomales Point) along the sea cliffs from Mc-Clures Beach north, and along the eastern side of the peninsula at Tomales Bay.

In the story of the peninsula's vertical movements, even clearer than the evidence of the rocks are the clues to be found in the forms and shapes of the land. Perhaps the most spectacular piece of evidence is visible at the south end

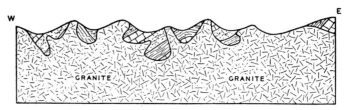

D. Partial erosion of metamorphosed rock exposed granite leaving pendants of former roof rock.

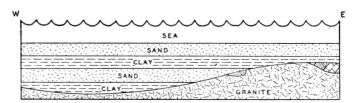

E. Granite was covered by layers of new sediments when ocean covered the land.

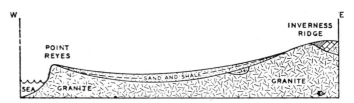

F. Granite again exposed by wind and water erosion of sediments following reëmergence of land mass.

of the peninsula. Covering an area of several square miles is a relatively flat region some 140 to 160 feet above the ocean—Bolinas Mesa. Such a flat area is rare in an otherwise mountainous region and when found near the ocean is almost certainly the remnant of an old marine terrace.

At some time in the past 10 million years when the peninsula was lower or the sea higher, the waves met the land above what is now the mesa. The ocean surf battered away at the land, carving away the edge of the hills to create a sea cliff. Just below the level of the attacking waves, there was left a smooth terrace.

As you look now from Bolinas across the mesa, the bed of an ancient sea, you can discern at the upper end of the mesa the steep hillsides which were once sea cliffs, now eroded by wind and rain into gentler slopes. Above them,

The Great Beach

Drake's Beach

along the top of the ridge, are the smooth hills that had been eroded into rounded shapes during some earlier epoch. Thus although the ridge has fairly steep sides, eroded by the ocean and by streams cutting into it, for most of its length the top of the ridge is surprisingly rounded—the remains of the old erosion surface.

THE BIG THAW

After the formation of the broad wave-cut terrace, the land slowly rose once again, rolling back the ocean and leaving the terrace high and dry. Once again the elements went to work, wearing away the old sea cliffs, spreading part of the cut-away soil and rocks over the terrace, cutting shallow valleys into the mesa itself.

During the great Ice Age, when much of the earth's water was congealed in the ice sheet covering much of the Northern Hemisphere, sea level was possibly 400 feet lower than it is today, and it was doubtless during this period, covering most of the past million years, that the present shallow valleys were carved. At that time the coastline was at least several miles farther out, making the peninsula far larger. It is probable that the streams flowing southward from this area continued until they flowed into the Sacramento River, which then entered the lowered ocean some miles west of the present Golden Gate.

Beginning some 25,000 years ago, the great ice sheets began to melt, and sea level rose steadily. It entered the river-carved Golden Gate and invaded an inland valley to form San Francisco Bay. And eventually it entered the Olema Valley—which had been eroded along the fault zone, occupying the ends of the valley to create Bolinas Lagoon and Tomales Bay. Waves of the rising sea battered the shoreline around the entire perimeter, forming new sea cliffs and cutting them back until they reached their present location. Below the cliffs, most conspicuously at Duxbury Reef, the waves have created a new wave-cut platform, exposed to the air for a half-mile seaward at times of very low tides.

But the story of the up and down movements of this peninsula is not yet complete. At some time very recently, probably within the past several thousand years, there has been another vertical movement, this time a downwarping. In response to the same rhythms of rise and fall that had acted on this land for millions of years, the bedrock between Inverness Ridge and Point Reyes has sagged into a syncline, until parts of the area were below sea level and invaded by the ocean. The drowned valleys that resulted are Drakes and Limantour esteros and Abbotts Lagoon.

This downwarping is dramatically visible along the coastline immediately north of Bear Valley. Here the old wave-cut terrace that is exposed farther south as Bolinas Mesa is much narrower and largely covered by sediments washed down from Inverness Ridge, forming a shelf above the ocean for several miles. The shelf gradually slopes down to the northwest until it reaches the beach and disappears beneath the sands of Drakes Bay, and dips beneath the esteros, forming the syncline.

Other evidence of this sinking of the central part of the peninsula can be seen on the map. Beyond the point where the old terrace disappears beneath the sand, the lower ends of the canyons opening on Drakes Bay have been

Drake's Beach

Seals and rocks

invaded by the ocean to form drowned valleys. In each of five successive canyons from east to west the sea has penetrated farther, indicating greater sinking, until the maximum penetration of about four miles at Drakes Estero marks the low point of the downwarping.

THE GREAT BEACH

The most recent chapter in the development of the major land forms of this peninsula concerns the formation of the beaches. The most rapidly changing features of the earth's crust are the transient margins of the great oceans. They adapt themselves rapidly to changes of sea level, land elevation, and even the works of man.

There are few more spectacular strands on this continent than the Great Beach sweeping along the ocean 11 miles north from the Point Reyes light in an unbroken line of dunes, white beach sand, and breakers.

Offshore, the ocean waves, driven by the prevailing northwest wind, sweep southward, carrying with them great quantities of sand that they have carved from the coastal cliffs. Much of the sand deposited on this beach has been quarried by the waves from the cliffs of Tomales Point, where the old granite bedrock is exposed to the surf's attacks. Off the cliffs hundreds of sea stacks— and other rock remnants which were recently part of the cliffs—testify to the rapidity with which this shoreline is being consumed by the waves and the resulting sand deposited along the Great Beach to the south.

Exposed directly to the strong northwest winds, which blow here almost directly onshore, the sand of the beach is carried above the backshore and deposited in rows of undulating dunes extending hundreds of yards inland. In the low area around Abbotts Lagoon the sand has been blown more than half a mile inland and in one area north of the lagoon the wind has deposited continuous dunes to a distance of a full mile from the beach.

Sand-laden waves have deposited a bar across the entrance to the lagoon, damming it off from the ocean. High tides and storm waves override the bar and winter rains usually will cause the lagoon to overflow into the ocean, cutting a channel that lasts until the bar is built up again.

Sweeping on southward past Point Reyes with their burden of sand, the long lines of swells moving in from the Pacific are diffracted around the point until some of them are rolling from the east toward the inner side of the promontory—a complete turn-about.

The diffracted waves deposit part of their load of sand along the southward-facing shore, creating the broad beaches of Drakes Bay. Just as the waves at Abbotts Lagoon created a bar that dammed off the lagoon from the ocean, so the waves at Drakes Bay have sealed off the entrances to all but the largest esteros. Only the tidal flow of water in and out of Drakes and Limantour esteros keeps the entrance from being completely closed off by three-mile-long Limantour Spit, one of the longest sand bars on the Pacific Coast.

All sand beaches are sensitive to the slightest shifts in waves, winds, and tides and consequently undergo changes in size and shape from year to year, season to season, and even from tide to tide. In general, beaches are built up by the gentle waves of summer and cut away by the large waves of winter. During winter storms many of the beaches below the white cliffs of Drakes Bay may

Tidepool, McClure's Beach

be entirely swept away, revealing the rocks beneath. Sand accumulations of many years can be swept away in a single storm. Then the beach is slowly restored over a period of months or years. Studies of the entrance to Drakes Estero by the Drake Navigators Guild indicate that there may be fairly regular cycles in the formation and shaping of the entrance.

Fortunately, man has as yet made few alterations in the land forms of this peninsula. One of his changes has been largely accidental. Early ranchers cleared or burned away great expanses of brush on the rolling hills to provide fields for planting and grassy pastures for their cattle. The crops and grasses were unable to hold the soil and over the decades great quantities of it have washed down into the bays and esteros. As a result Drakes Estero is doubtless far shallower than it was in Drake's time, and considerably shallower than it was even in the early decades of this century when sailing schooners put in at its docks to transport produce and dairy products to San Francisco. Similar shoaling has occurred in Bolinas Lagoon, and Tomales Bay, too, has been filled at the upper end, partly by erosion deposits, partly by the construction of levees to drain the marshes. Commercial vessels once regularly operated as far south as White House Pool at Inverness Park, two miles above the present head of the bay.

THE GEOLOGIC FUTURE

Just as this peninsula provides a means of looking into the seemingly endless vistas of the geologic past, so it offers opportunity for views into a far-distant future.

A glimpse into such a future can be a staggering experience. Having confronted the vast magnitude of time past, the human mind tends to take comfort in the assumption that the past is but a prelude to the present and that the geologic processes have at last, in our time, reached their ultimate point of development. But to contemplate the future as well is to confront squarely the fact that the span of time encompassed by a single life is but a split second of time as measured by the processes of the earth.

The future is seldom a matter of certainty, but by projecting present earth processes it is possible to develop a conception of probabilities.

The probabilities are greatest in terms of those processes that are taking place so rapidly that their action can be observed over a period of years. Aside from the continuous alterations in the changeable beaches, the processes occurring most rapidly are the filling of the bays and the erosion of the cliffs. Bolinas Lagoon and upper Tomales Bay will relatively soon be dry land, speaking in geologic time. The retreat of the cliffs before the attacks of the waves is most rapid in the Bolinas area, where the sandstone is less resistant than in other areas and the average rate of cutback is about a foot a year. The most vivid example is at Duxbury Point, where a section of clifftop road built during the 1920s has long since disappeared, leaving the severed ends hanging high.

Should Bolinas Mesa become heavily built over, doubtless the rate of cliff retreat would be speeded. As has occurred in many clifftop subdivisions, water from lawns and gardens has saturated the subsoil until it drains out through the cliffs, causing slides, particularly in places where the bluffs have already been undermined by wave attack.

Even without such artificially caused slides, the cutting back of the cliffs

Jack rabbit

can be expected to continue until Bolinas Mesa is cut away and the ocean stands once again below the remains of ancient cliffs it carved millions of years ago.

On the other hand, an elevation of the land, such as the uplift that raised the ancient sea cliffs far above the ocean, would again roll the ocean back, spare the mesa and leave the present cliffs to tower above a new mesa, formed by the present low-tide terrace. New cliffs would be eroded into the new mesa some distance farther out. The same result would ensue if the land remained stationary and the sea level retreated in some new ice age.

The cliffs that reminded Drake of his homeland are also retreating. Possibly even more rapid than the cutback of these cliffs, will be the changes in the land caused by the surf's battering away at the foot of the landslides which formed the lakes farther south. This jumble of rocks is doomed to become even more chaotic as the waves undermine the foot of the slides, causing more rock debris from above to tumble down to the ocean.

VANISHED LAND

The most dramatic example of the action of the waves in cutting away the land is at Point Reyes itself. Even in a region of highly abnormal geology, this piece of land is clearly extraordinary. Approach it from the north and it looms like a massive island over the low rolling hills and sunken valleys of the esteros. Clearly it belongs to another segment of time.

Along the northern boundaries of this promontory, where it rises above the lowlands, there are whale fossils and signs of an ancient beach hundreds of feet above sea level. Here, evidently, was a shore of an ancient inland sea, protected by some vanished headland or peninsula from the direct attacks of the surf.

Continue beyond the ancient beach line southward as the ridge rises to a high point of more than 500 feet. Suddenly the land drops off in a sharp escarpment and you confront the roaring ocean, as far below as if you were standing on top of a 40-story building. It is evident that at some distant time in the past, before these cliffs were formed, the ground continued to rise southward and formed a huge land mass which has since been eroded away by the ocean. Look southward on a clear day and you can see some 20 miles offshore the rocky isles of the Farallones, the barren rock nubs of that same land mass—formed of the same granite that the waves have exposed here at the point.

If the wave attacks continue, these last remnants will themselves disappear, consumed by the omnivorous Pacific like the vanished land mass to which they once belonged.

The disappearance of Point Reyes will be hastened greatly if the sinking of the land in the estero area continues. Sooner or later Drakes Estero will break through to the Great Beach, and Point Reyes will again become an island, subject, like the Farallones, to wave attack on the north as well as the south.

THE POINTING FINGER

At the north end of the peninsula is another remnant of a land feature that has disappeared. Stand on Tomales Point looking north across Bodega Bay

Inverness Ridge

Drake's Beach

and you see the hulking mass of Bodega Head five miles away. Tomales Point seems to be a long finger pointing directly at that high promontory. The direction is significant. The San Andreas fault extends north out of Tomales Bay and across Bodega Bay, cutting off Bodega Head. The head itself, unlike the rock east of the fault, is composed of the same kind of granite that forms the base of this peninsula and is exposed in the cliffs of Tomales Point.

At some unknown time in the past the granite of Tomales Point evidently extended across the five miles to Bodega Head, and the two promontories were part of the same ridge. Over the millenniums the ocean apparently battered its way entirely through the ridge and entered the valley which had been created by the great fault, flooding the fault zone to create Tomales and Bodega bays.

From the standpoint of the geologic future, Tomales Point is ominously thin. Along its west side the ocean continues to erode back the sea cliffs, leaving the offshore stacks and rocks that are signs of a rapid cutback. Streams cutting their way into the eastern side of the ridge are transporting great quantities of it into Tomales Bay, and the tidal currents of the bay itself continually erode back the granite bluffs along that side.

There are few more vivid demonstrations of the power of a pounding surf than here where it has removed innumerable millions of tons of granite. The question as to what happened to the granite that formed this linking ridge can be answered by a look at the shoreline immediately to the south. Most of that rock, digested into granules by the omnivorous ocean and distributed southward by the prevailing winds and waves, now forms the sand on the Great Beach. That beach, oddly enough, is considerably more permanent than the granite cliffs, for although much of it is removed by wind and storm, it is continually replenished by quantities of sand quarried by the waves from the cliffs of the point.

Other things being equal, it might be expected that the narrow finger of land culminating in Tomales Point will be shortened inch by inch and mile by mile, ground into sand by the waves, until the surf washes ashore on what is now the eastern side of Tomales Bay.

Yet other things are never equal. It may be that long before the thin north end of the peninsula is worn away, another ice age will cause sea level to drop and the ocean to retreat, carving a new shoreline on what is now sea bottom many miles to the west. Or the continued melting of polar ice might result in a rise of sea level and the inundation of the lowlands. The peninsula itself may rise or sink or be thrust many miles farther to the north along the great fault, cast into completely new shapes.

The only certainty is that this exceedingly mobile section of the earth's crust will continue to change in unpredictable ways. Man can only stand on this threshold and peer with wonder a short distance into spans of time inconceivably greater than the span of his own life and, very probably, that of his species.

Prospect

I T IS A FOGGY TWILIGHT at Drakes Bay, and as you walk through the rolling dunes of Limantour Spit the dark misty shape of Point Reyes is barely visible across the water. The only sounds are the boom of the breakers and the occasional cries of the shore birds. The tide is very low. Sky, dunes, and ocean are varying shades of gray; only the glistening sand underfoot seems to hold the last light of the day. Long sinuous sea plants are left on the sand's smooth surface by the retreating tide.

At the water's edge several stiff-legged sandpipers probe the sand with their elongated bills, then, as you approach, rise with a sweep of wings and long piercing whistle, circle wide over the surf and return to the beach a hundred yards ahead. A flock of small round sanderlings dart in and out with each wave like gray and white balls rolling swiftly back and forth in advance of the water.

Toward the end of the long sandspit you hear the sound of flowing water. Here the beach turns inland. The tide is ebbing and all the waters of the esteros are racing swiftly seaward through this channel like a river whose far shore is barely visible in the gathering darkness.

At high water, the breakers roll in through this channel, roiling it to white, then disappear in the calm waters of the esteros. But now, on a minus tide, the waves are breaking on a bar far out beyond the entrance and their distant roar is barely audible above the rush of the ebbing waters of the channel.

Suddenly you hear in front of you a loud splash, as if some heavy object had been thrown into the water. Then you make out in the misty twilight the head of a sea lion staring up at you as it sweeps past on the ebb. The big mammal heaves part way out of the water, then submerges with another splash and reappears a few yards away. Then another brown head comes by, and this one, too, stares curiously at the odd interloper on this deserted beach.

It occurs to you that the ancestors of these same sea mammals may have similarly gazed at the men of Drake on that long distant day when the *Golden Hind* landed, perhaps just across the channel from where you stand.

Out in the channel itself you can discern a significant sight. With the ebbing tide, several large sand bars have appeared. They seem to have risen from the water like newly created continents. Could such a bar be the mysterious "island" pictured on contemporary maps of Drake's unknown landing place? Is this the key to the lost harbor of the *Golden Hind?*

The sounds you hear now on this beach in the twilight—the flowing water and the pounding surf, the plaintive cry of a plover, the bark of the sea lions— are the sounds heard by the men of Drake and the men of Cermeño, and you can envision the light of their campfires glowing on the far cliffs and hear in imagination the talk and songs of lonesome men on an alien shore half a world away from home.

As you stand here the ebbing current is cutting terraces and escarpments in the sand. There is a four-foot sand cliff at your feet, and the moving water slices away at its edges. Several inches of cliff tumble into the current, forcing you to step back. Here is vivid evidence of the way beaches and bars change contours on every tide, just as the continents in the long epochs of geologic evolution change shapes when the sea alternately invades them and is rolled back.

On this lonely shore in the darkness you confront not only the centuries of man's time on this continent but the vastly greater stretches of time in the workings of the elemental processes of the earth, the carving of the coastlines, the creation of islands and wave-cut cliffs and terraces, the primeval rhythms of the rising and falling seas.

You confront still more. Mingled with the sound of the surf you can almost hear another far-off roar, the sound of the approaching tides of humanity. For the incoming tide that began with the first explorers is now, four centuries later, rapidly rising to the maximum flood.

Elsewhere in this burgeoning metropolitan region long rows of houses are covering the rolling hillsides. Shorelines are bulldozed and bulwarked into city lots. The subdivisions, the shopping centers, the freeways, the asphalt deserts of parking lots are obliterating the last of the natural landscapes. There will be few remaining places where it will be possible to escape the epidemic of urbanization, the relentless advance of concrete and chrome and cold glaring neon.

You find yourself hoping fervently that the swarming millions of future residents of this region will cherish this island in time and other enclaves of nature, will resist all encroachment by the bulldozers that come in the name of progress and profits. You pray that your grandchildren's generation—and their descendants for centuries to come—will be able to find here solitude on an unspoiled beach, the renewal of body and spirit that comes from contact with the natural forms and rhythms of the earth. You hope devoutly that they, too, may have the opportunity to wander here alone and to listen to the throaty roar of the sea lion, the cry of the plover, the soft sound of the wind through the beach grass of the sand dunes.

The last light leaves the flowing water and the flat sands, and you walk slowly back in the misty gloom along the beach. All sounds now seem heightened in the darkness, and you can detect in the roar of the surf the varied tones of the moving water, the resonant boom of the swell breaking into a wave, the turbulent churning of the incoming comber, the diminishing rush of the spent wave spreading itself on the sand at your feet, then the whisper of the slack water retreating to begin again the immemorial cycle that Sophocles heard long ago on the Aegean. From somewhere out in the darkness comes the cry of a shore bird, sad slow notes in a minor mode . . .

About the Sierra Club

The Sierra Club, founded in 1892 by John Muir, has devoted itself to the study and protection of the nation's scenic and ecological resources—mountains, wetlands, woodlands, wild shores and rivers. All club publications are part of the nonprofit effort the club carries on as a public trust. There are 42 chapters coast to coast, in Canada, Hawaii and Alaska. Participation is invited in the club's program to enjoy and preserve wilderness everywhere. Address: 1050 Mills Tower, San Francisco, California 94104; 597 Fifth Avenue, New York, N.Y. 10017, or 324 "C" Street, S.E., Washington, D.C. 20002.